ATOM AND MOLECULES

CHEMISTRY BOOK GRADE 4

CHILDREN'S CHEMISTRY BOOKS

BABY PROFESSOR
EDUCATION KIDS

Speedy Publishing LLC

40 E. Main St. #1156

Newark, DE 19711

www.speedypublishing.com

Laboratory test tubes and flasks with colored liquids on the periodic table of elements.

Chemistry involves the study of properties of matter and how that matter interacts with the energy that surrounds it. It is considered to be a physical science and related to physics. It is also referred to as the "Central Science" since it is a dire part of the other sciences including physics, biology, and Earth science. A scientist specializing in chemistry is known as a chemist.

Read further to learn about atoms and molecules and how they work together.

ATOM STRUCTURE

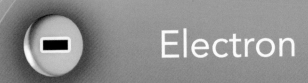 Electron

 Neutron

 Proton

THE ATOM

This is the basic of all matter. They are very small and consist of even tinier particles. Neutrons, Protons, and Electrons are the basic particles making up the atom. They join together with other atoms and create matter. It takes many atoms to create anything. The human body is made up of so many that it is almost impossible to write the number down. Probably somewhere in the trillions. The different atoms are created from the number of neutrons, protons, and electrons that is contained in each atom.

Each different type represents an element. There are 92 elements in their natural form, and up to 118 if you include the elements that are man-made. For the most part, they can last forever. They have the ability to change and also undergo chemical reactions, by sharing electrons with the other atoms. The nucleus is difficult to split, which means that most of them hang around for a very long time.

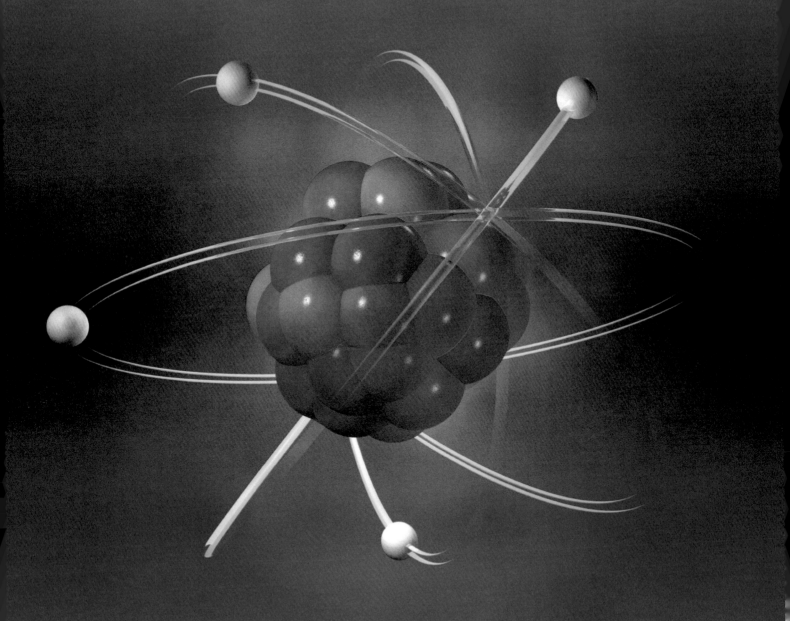

Atom Structure

STRUCTURE OF THE ATOM

Its center is known as the nucleus. It consists of neutrons and protons. Its electron's spin in orbits that surround the nucleus.

THE PROTON

The particle that is positively charged at its center is known as the nucleus. The hydrogen is one of a kind since it contains only one proton and no neutron.

ATOM

Nucleus

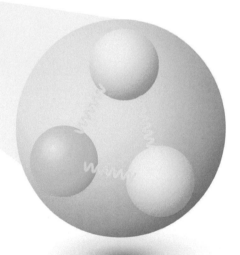

PROTON

ATOM

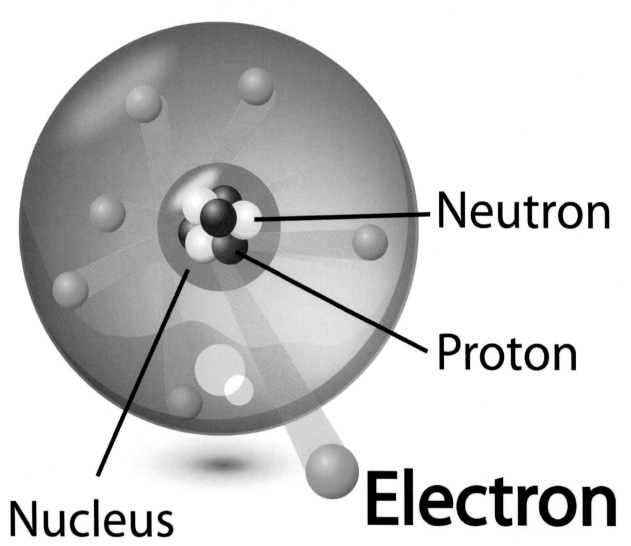

Neutron

Proton

Nucleus

Electron

THE ELECTRON

The negatively charged particle that spins outside the nucleus is known as the electron. They spin so quickly around its nucleus that scientists cannot be 100% sure as to their location. If an atom contains the same number of protons and neutrons, it is considered to have a neutral charge. The electrons are pulled to the atom's nucleus by the positive charge provided by its protons. They are smaller than protons and neutrons. Around 1800 times as small!

THE NEUTRON

Particles in an atom having a neutral charge are known as neutrons. They are neither positive or negative. That does not mean that they do not play a major role in it. Each part of an atom is necessary for it to behave and act as it does. This includes the neutrons.

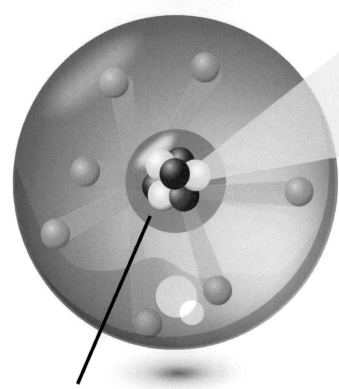

ATOM

NEUTRON

Nucleus

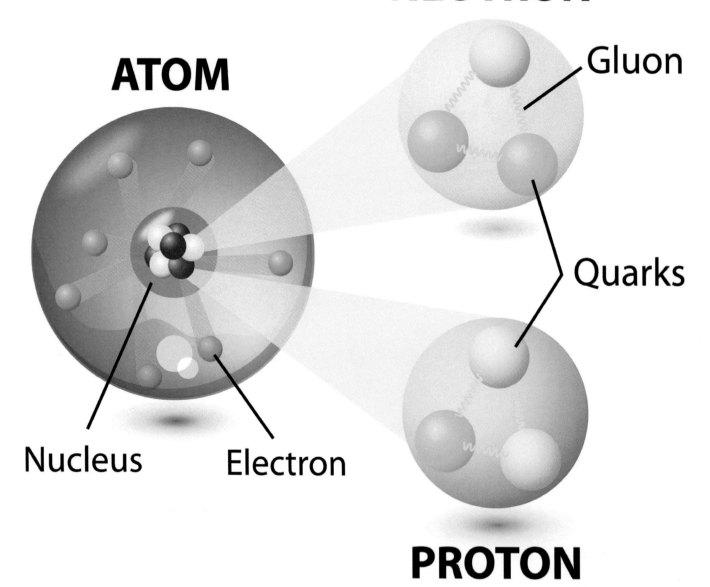

ATOM

NEUTRON

Gluon

Quarks

PROTON

Nucleus

Electron

OTHER PARTICLES

QUARK – These are tiny particles that create the protons and neutrons. Quarks are almost impossible to notice and were only recently discovered, in 1964 by Murray Gell-Mann.

There are six different types: top, bottom, up, down, strange, and charm.

NEUTRINO – Nuclear reactions create neutrinos. They are similar to electrons that don't have a charge and usually they travel at the speed of light. The sun emits more than a trillion of neutrinos each second. They have the ability to pass through a solid object, including the human body.

Standard Model of Elementary Particles

		Fermions			Bosons
mass → charge → spin → name →	Quarks	2.4 MeV/c² ⅔ ½ u up	1.27 GeV/c² ⅔ ½ c charm	171.2 GeV/c² ⅔ ½ t top	0 0 1 γ photon
	Quarks	4.8 MeV/c² -⅓ ½ d down	104 MeV/c² -⅓ ½ s strange	4.2 GeV/c² -⅓ ½ b bottom	0 0 1 g gluon
	Leptons	<2.2 eV/c² 0 ½ ν_e muon neutrino	<0.17 MeV/c² 0 ½ ν_μ muon neutrino	<15.5 MeV/c² 0 ½ ν_τ muon neutrino	91.2 GeV/c² 0 1 Z^0 Z boson
	Leptons	0.511 MeV/c² -1 ½ e electron	105.7 MeV/c² -1 ½ μ muon	1.777 GeV/c² -1 ½ τ tau	80.4 GeV/c² ±1 1 $W^{\pm}$ W boson
Three Generations of Matter (Fermions) →		I	II	III	

DNA Molecule

MOLECULES

When two atoms join, they create a molecule. Everything around consists of molecules, including the human body. The human body actually consists of more than trillions of various types of molecules.

COMPOUNDS

When atoms of different types join, they create molecules known as compounds. Water is made of compound molecules consisting of 2 hydrogen and 1 oxygen atoms. That is why it is referred to as H_2O. Water will always consist of two times the amount of hydrogen as its oxygen atoms.

H₂O
Water

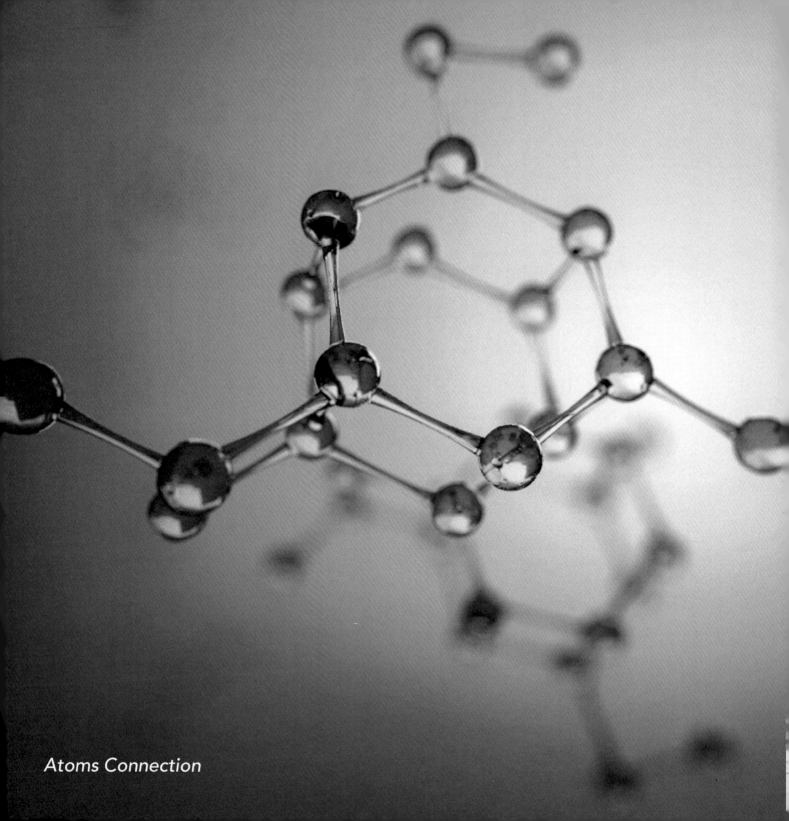

Atoms Connection

HOW ARE COMPOUNDS NAMED?

Chemists follow specific rules in naming compounds, and scientists all over the world follow these same standards when naming a compound. A compounds name is structured from its elements and molecular construction.

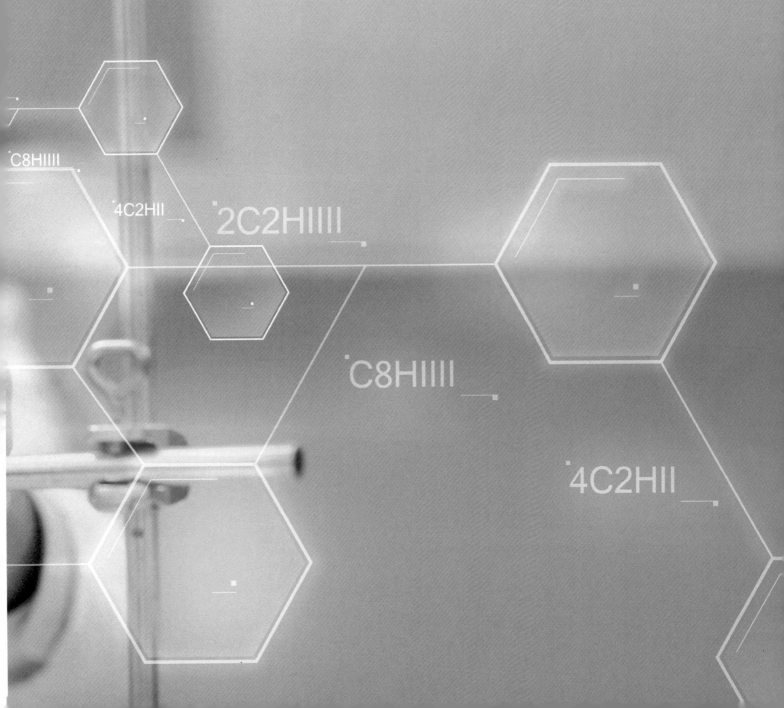
Close up of scientist filling test tubes with funnel and doing research in clinical laboratory

MOLECULAR FORMULA

While there may only be a few more than 100 different types of atoms, there are many millions of substances. This happens since they all consist of different molecules. Not only are molecules made of the different types of atoms, but there are different ratios as well. Remember discussing water earlier? A water molecule consists of 2 hydrogen molecules and 1 oxygen atom, written as H_2O.

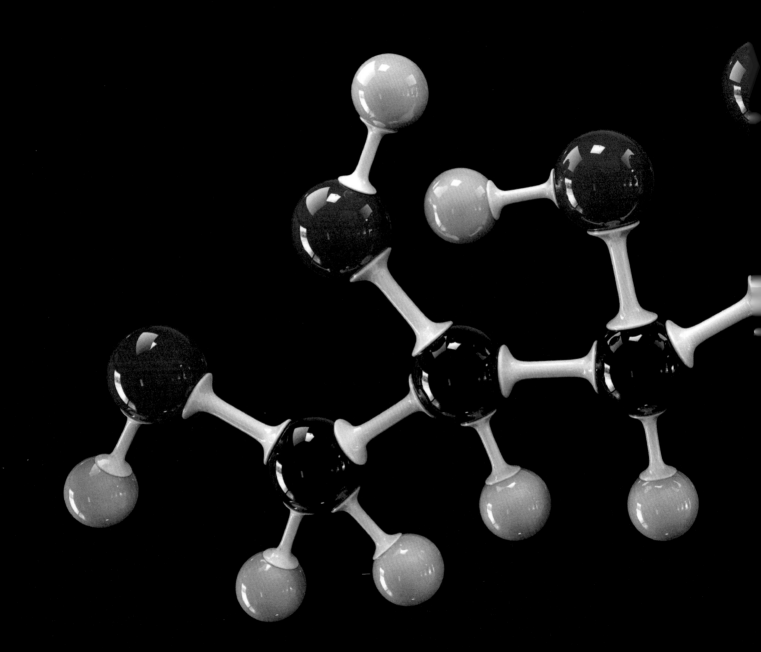

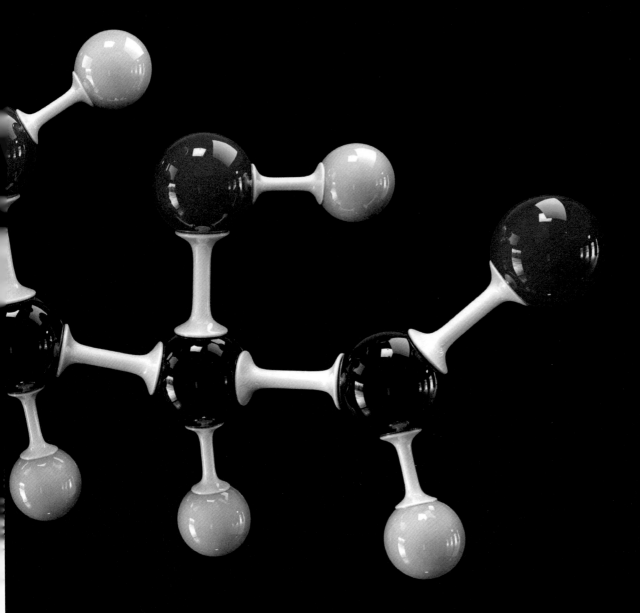

molecule of **Glucose**

3D Illustration

C6H12O6

Some other examples would be ammonia (NH_3), carbon dioxide (CO_2), and glucose or sugar ($C_6H_{12}O_6$). Some of these formulas can get to be complex and long. Let's take a look at sugar: C_6 - 6 carbon atoms, H_{12} - 12 hydrogen atoms, and O_6 - 6 oxygen atoms. These atoms have to contain these specific numbers to create a molecule of sugar.

Molecules can have various shapes. While some may be in the shape of a pyramid, some appear to be long spirals.

FORMATION OF OZONE

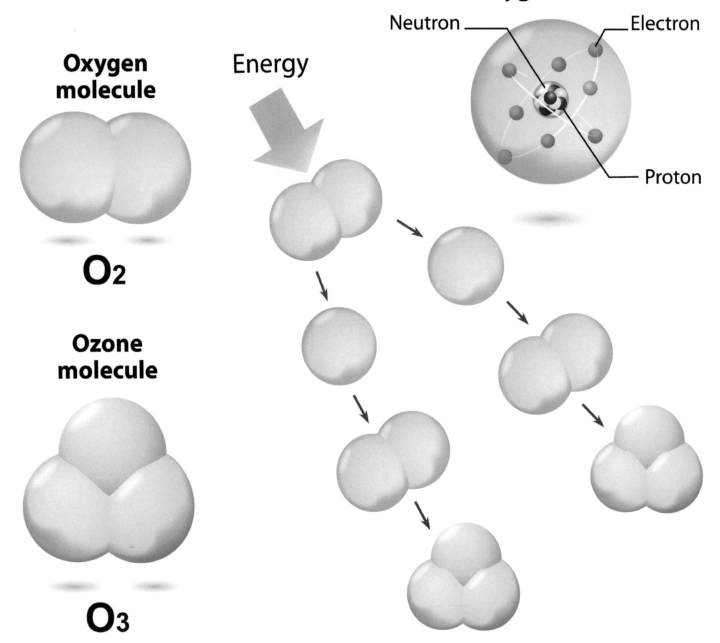

Oxygen gas typically has the molecule O_2, but can also be O_3 which is referred to as ozone.

Compounds containing carbon are known as organic compounds.

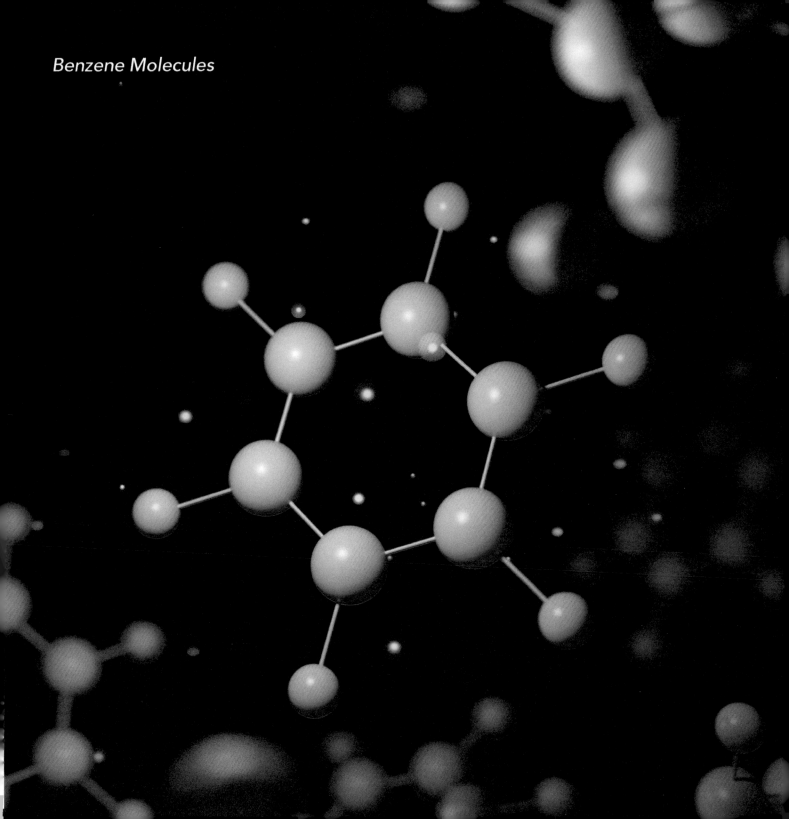

Benzene Molecules

DNA Molecule Spiral

Have you heard the term DNA? DNA is a really long molecule containing information which is unique to every human being.

BONDS

Molecules and compounds are held together with chemical bonds. Most compounds are held together by two types of bonds: Ionic bonds and Covalent bonds. Certain compounds may be held together by both ionic and covalent bonds.

Metallic bonding and properties

Metallic bonding

Sea of delocalised electrons

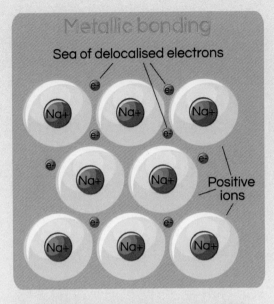

Positive ions

Electrical conductivity

Thermal conductivity

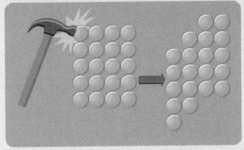

Malleability

Ductility

Crystal lattices

Cubic face centered (fcc)   Cubic body centered (bcc)   Hexagonal close packed (hcp)

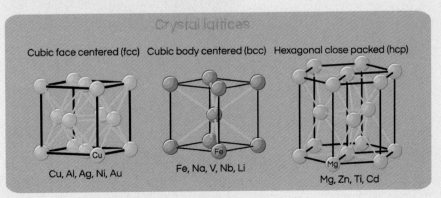

Cu

Fe

Mg

Cu, Al, Ag, Ni, Au   Fe, Na, V, Nb, Li   Mg, Zn, Ti, Cd

Shiny texture

These two main bonds involve electrons, and they orbit the atoms. The shells need to be "full" of the electrons. If they are not full, they try to bond with different atoms to get to the correct number of electrons.

COVALENT BONDS - These bonds share their electrons between different atoms. This occurs when atoms share electrons to fill the outer shell.

IONIC BONDS - These bonds form as one electron is donated to another atom. This occurs when it gives away an electron to another one to form a balance and a compound or molecule.

CHEMICAL BONDING

Atoms consist of very small units of matter.

Everything around us is made from very small units of matter referred to as atoms. Chemical bonding is the process used to make atoms join together forming substances.

CHEMICAL BONDING

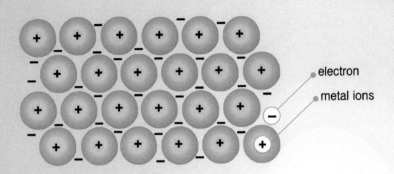

electron

metal ions

Metallic Bonding

Hydrogen
Bond

Hydrogen Bonding

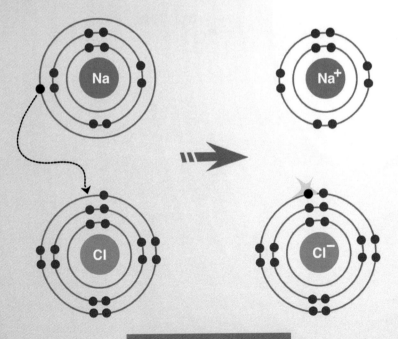

Na

Cl

Na⁺

Cl⁻

İonic Bonding

Electron from
carbon

Electron from
hydrogen

H

H

C

H

H

Covalent Bonding

ATOMS

As you learned earlier, every element contains a unique atom consisting of a certain number of protons located at its nucleus known as the atomic number. They also each have the same number of electrons and protons.

When a lot of atoms lose their electrons, this is known as metallic bonding.

Atoms contained in molecules are joined by an attraction between the shared electrons and the nucleus.

Atom with nucleus, atomic shell and orbiting electrons

ELECTRON SHELLS

As the electron shells orbit the nucleus of its atom, they remain in layers known as shells. Every shell is only able to contain a precise amount of electrons. Its first layers holds two electrons, the next layer eight, the third layer holds 18, and so on.

THE OUTER SHELL

While every atom wants a full outer shell, only the noble gases naturally contains a full outer shell. These gases are located on the right of the periodic table. Thus, as atoms that do contain a full outer shell encounter other atoms, they want to gain or give up electrons.

Since the outer shell of the noble gases are full naturally, there is seldom a reaction.

NOBLE GASES

18   **Argon**   Ar   2   **Helium**   He

Atomic mass: 39.948
Electron configuration: 2, 8, 8

Atomic mass: 4.0026
Electron configuration: 2

36   **Krypton**   Kr   10   **Neon**   Ne

Atomic mass: 83.798
Electron configuration: 2, 8,18,8

Atomic mass: 20.179
Electron configuration: 2, 8

VALENCE ELECTRONS

The amount of electrons in the outer shell that have the ability to form chemical bonds with the other atoms are known as valence electrons.

Atoms that have a somewhat empty outer shell want to give up their electrons. An example would be if it contains 1 electron out of 8 possible electrons, it then wants to give away the 1 electron so that its outer shell is full.

When its almost full, it will need additional electrons to fill its outer shell. An example would be an atom containing 6 out of 8 electrons will want to add 2 to fill its outer shell.

IONIC BONDING

This occurs as one element gives an electron (electrons) to another filling the outer shell of both elements.

Ionic bonding typically occurs between metals which are located to the left of the periodic table.

Ionic bonding

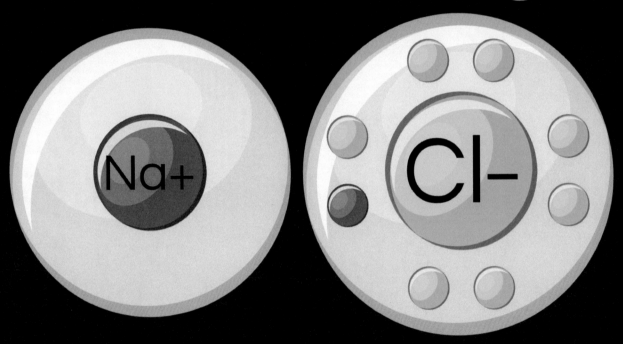

Nonpolar covalent bonding

Polar covalent bonding

COVALENT BONDING

This occurs when the one atom shares electrons rather than giving or taking them to fill their outer shells. The electrons always share in pairs.

THE PERIODIC TABLE OF ELEMENTS

The Periodic Table is how the elements are listed. The elements are listed by their atomic structure, which includes the number of protons and the number of electrons contained in their outer shell. They are listed left to right and top to bottom in order by their atomic number, the number of protons contained in each atom.

There is so much more to learn about solutions and chemistry. For additional information on Chemical Solutions, you can research the internet, go to your local library, and ask questions of your teachers, family, and friends.

Visit

BABY PROFESSOR
EDUCATION KIDS

www.BabyProfessorBooks.com

to download Free Baby Professor eBooks
and view our catalog of new and exciting
Children's Books